The Phoenix Living Poets

A HOUSE OF VOICES

Poets Published in
The Phoenix Living Poets Series

★

JAMES AITCHISON
ALEXANDER BAIRD · ALAN BOLD
R. H. BOWDEN · FREDERICK BROADIE
GEORGE MACKAY BROWN
PHILIP CALLOW · HAYDEN CARRUTH
JOHN COTTON · JENNIFER COUROUCLI
GLORIA EVANS DAVIES
PATRIC DICKINSON
TOM EARLEY · D. J. ENRIGHT
IRENE FEKETE
JOHN FULLER · DAVID GILL
PETER GRUFFYDD
J. C. HALL · MOLLY HOLDEN
JOHN HORDER · P. J. KAVANAGH
RICHARD KELL · LAURIE LEE
LAURENCE LERNER
CHRISTOPHER LEVENSON
EDWARD LOWBURY · NORMAN MACCAIG
ROY MCFADDEN
JON MANCHIP WHITE
DIANA MCLOGHLEN
JAMES MERRILL · RUTH MILLER
LESLIE NORRIS · ROBERT PACK
ARNOLD RATTENBURY
ADRIENNE RICH · JON SILKIN
JON STALLWORTHY
GILLIAN STONEHAM
EDWARD STOREY · TERENCE TILLER
SYDNEY TREMAYNE
LOTTE ZURNDORFER

A HOUSE
OF VOICES

By

J. C. HALL

CHATTO AND WINDUS

THE HOGARTH PRESS

1973

Published by
Chatto & Windus Ltd
with The Hogarth Press Ltd
42 William IV Street
London W.C.2

Distributed in the United States of America
by Wesleyan University Press

63063

ISBN 7011 1913 6

Printed in Great Britain by
Lewis Reprints Ltd
The Brown Knight & Truscott Group
London and Tonbridge

CONTENTS

TO MUE

*The author is grateful to the Arts Council
for a grant that enabled him to give more
time than would have otherwise been possible
to the writing of these poems.*

SPEECH AFTER LONG SILENCE

At school I arranged the time
Of my daily piano stint
To avoid the personal dole
(The master took the hint,
Bless him) of stammering through
The scriptural rigmarole.

I don't know who blushed the more,
I or the others there,
When Abraham stuck on my tongue
And I couldn't get out the name
Of the first disciple and hung
Jesus up, to my shame.

So I murdered Chopin instead
Hating that lesson too.
Better a tripped-up scale
Than a glottal stop I said.
When Music came to an end
I hardly knew what to do.

Things are easier now.
Sometimes I stick when tired
Or very drunk, but I flow
Reasonably well and get
Business and pleasure done
Without being dropped or fired.

An allegory of the Muse?
Let's leave it I suffer gaps
When nothing comes, whole years
Of poetry out of use.
Now that I'm bubbling along
I may keep it up perhaps.

APRIL THE FIRST

'A certain irony' my father said
    Five years ago, and what he meant
Still puzzles me. I cannot see the thread
    Between the tom-fool day you went

And what you were. Naked, perhaps our grief
    Needs distancing. A wry remark
Covers the public wound and brings relief
    Until the privacy of the dark.

Irony, no. But still this day each year,
    Being unique itself, has set
Firm in my calendar all that you were,
    And are — for how can I forget?

THE GENERATIONS

It is not I but my younger daughter
Props up the likeness of you I brought her
Back from your death and the turning-out
Of your memory hoard. What a sad disquiet
Of uncles and aunts and distant cousins
And me looking sulky on odd occasions
That was. And the stabbing sight of your hand
So firmly chronicling 'Margate' and
'Twenty-something' (those timeless summers)
And 'Blanche' on the back of Mrs. Chalmers.
A lot got chucked. 'These magpie women'
My father grunted, and perhaps for him in
Those desolate days such ruthless weeding
Of all that photographic inbreeding
Was just as well — made moving lighter
And your image, cleared of much moss, seem brighter.
'Take what you like.' Of the ones I chose
I've surrendered this calm Victorian pose,
Innocent-seeming, unbelievably good
(With all that fidgeting under the hood
And 'A little this way, miss, if you please'
You must have scowled). Now you sit at ease
Among her jars of cosmetical things
And travel trophies; and whose belongings
Are whose and the claims of the generations
Needs sharing, and love, and endless patience.

TWELVE MINUTES

The hearse comes up the road
With its funeral load

Sharp on the stroke of twelve.
I greet it myself,

Good-morning the head man
Who's brought the dead man.

I say we're four only.
Still, he won't be lonely.

Being next of kin
I'm the first one in

Behind the bearers,
The black mourning wearers.

(A quick thought appals:
What if one trips and falls?)

They lay him safely down,
The coffin a light brown.

Prayers begin. I sit
And let my mind admit

That screwed-down speechless thing
And how another spring

His spouse was carried here.
Now they're remarried here

And may be happier even
In the clean church of heaven.

We say the last amen.
A button's pressed and then

To canned funeral strains
His dear dead remains,

Eighty-four years gone by,
Sink with a whirring sigh.

I tip and say goodbye.

THE FORM

Today for the first time since you died
I travelled back. I sat in your chair
And saw the room as you'd seen it there,
The same things by the same fireside.

Or almost the same. The difference was
The vision opposite wasn't me.
The emptiness where I used to be
And talked and nodded and charged my glass

With the Special Blend you bought, confused
With the absence I presumed to fill
Simply by crossing the room until
Your sudden going was interfused

With my coming back as you had come,
After my visits, to sit and brood
On what I had said and the adulthood
That took me away to another home

And ways that could never be yours and yet
Were only mine because of the shape
Of the ways I learnt from your own lifescape
And habits picked up from your own mind-set.

Father and son — the equation holds
Enormous differences, close ties.
Only today did I see the lies
I muddled with truth in what I told.

As I sank back in the chair still warm
From your presence, I marvelled how we stay
And are most known when we go away
As the hare after it leaves its form.

AN EXCEPTIONAL MAY

I don't know what triggered it off.
The gin perhaps. He just sat there
In the garden on a fine May day
A week before his eighty-third year
And wept. There was nothing I could say.

I seemed to be eavesdropping on
A colloquy between one who'd died
And one who before May came again
Would leave a new ache in my side.
One or two words made plain

He was wandering back to the last time
And 'Good luck, old man' in Hammersmith
And the young feet walking away.
Then something began to give.
There was nothing that I could say.

So I went in and helped with the meal.
When I armed him in he was dry-eyed.
It was an exceptional May
The year before my father died.
Not a cloud. Just the sun all day.

A LETTER FROM THE SOMME

Date: fifty-four years ago almost to the day.
Place: not stated, but somewhere up the Somme.
Writer: a Colonel in the 10th Royal Fusiliers.
I have found this letter yellowed by the years
And learn of my father's gallantry, the way
He led his men to their almost certain doom.

He lost an eye and was invalided home.
Others 'less lucky' (wry note of fortitude)
Lost all the breath they had. Taylor and Bevis died,
Heathcote and Haviland were laid side by side
Not far from Hodding. They found Shurey room
In the same graveyard under a hanging wood.

He tots up the wounded next: Sharp, Campbell, Rees,
Armstrong, Proctor. Do some of these comrades live
Still, I wonder, with the memory of that day
When half the Company was blown away
Out of sheer hell into a sort of peace?
Reading this letter there's much I can't forgive,

Much that both makes and breaks my faith in man,
Much that becomes too much. These words that praise
A man for death and escaping death, the post
That brought such an elegy for each poor ghost —
Now I've survived fifty years of my span
I choke on the chance that chose me for these days.

A BURNING

The morning she brought the package down and said
'Please burn them,' I only hope my huge surprise
Didn't appear or make her feel ashamed
That now at last (or so it seemed) her grief
Had so digested every word and phrase
That to thumb through his letters still became
A dry indulgence. Laying aside my book
I took her sacrifice without a word.
'You don't mind, do you?' — I shook my head,
Not sure whether I minded but sure at least
That what I did and how I did it then
Meant, for us both, an end. I took them down —
Two hundred perhaps, all neatly tied, the news
Of school and barrack room, of how he'd come
Third in the class one week, and later found
Canada, where he trained, a friendly place,
And how after the war they'd take a cruise —
Took them behind the greenhouse out of sight
And shook them out like leaves. I doubt she saw
Anything of the blaze, and the thin smoke
Blew low over the hedge and scudded away
Down the valley. Some wouldn't catch. I raked
And prodded them with a fierce tenderness,
Coaxing his care to rest. For still his hand
Curled in the heat and words like negatives
Briefly stood out more boldly — his memory etched
On feathery fronds one moment, then breaking up
In fragile ruin.
                                    And when at last
Nothing but ash remained, I threw on earth
Like coffin-scatter, put back the hoe, went in
The kitchen way where, sharpening a knife,
She looked up, half-dismayed. I nodded, said
'They're gone,' matter-of-fact, and sat to eat
Whatever she'd cooked to keep us both alive.

RESOLUTIONS

We both made one, but did not know the other's.
I wondered what yours was. It's strange how near
One is, and yet how far, as brothers.
The first flake fluttered down into the year.

All day it fell. Slowly the world's traces —
Our footprints, birds' claws — vanished beneath those snows.
A curious light shone in on our faces.
O secret selves. White windows. The frost's rose.

THE MAGIC OF CHILDHOOD

After some quick-fire patter he takes six rings
And asks Penelope to check they're real,
Solid all round, no gaps. Pushing past Jane
She blushingly takes the one he offers, pings
It with her thumbnail, proves it's honest steel.
Hey presto! he's linked them like a daisy-chain.

Next, a billiard ball spawns into five
Between his fingers. From empty boxes
Handkerchiefs flower. He drags out yards and yards
Of coloured streamers, conjures up a live
But docile rabbit. All this magic foxes
Our young intelligence. Now playing cards

Are picked and guessed. 'Oh, I beg your pardon,
Look what's here!' He pulls a five pound note
Out of my pocket . . . I'm tiring of this game!
Slyly my interest wanders to the garden
Where all's in order: perennials full out,
Jock hoeing carrots, comfortably the same.

And all the time old Know-All softly mutters
'I'll tell you how it's done.' I say he mustn't,
Wanting my small illusions and my dreams.
Anyway, if he thinks the truth he utters
Has any relevance, I bet it doesn't.
Reality's never, never what it seems.

When Mrs. Kirk shepherds us to the meal
We squeeze the buns, wondering if they're real.

PONDS

When I was a boy I offered a reward
for the return of my comic if lost —
'One pond if found in the United
Kingdom, two ponds if found abroad'

Magnificent gesture! Splashes of nature free!
Had anyone claimed, insisting on the letter,
Some options were local then. Near Tunbridge Wells
I remember a beauty by a rotting mill.
At Crowborough, where clearly I hadn't learnt to spell,
A dew pond's discovered on the golf course still.

Eridge and Penshurst had some gems in stock.
Out Hawkhurst way one with a weeping willow.
And — can I mention it without colouring up? —
That treacherous one in Grandfather's meadow
They fished me from like some bedraggled pup,
The maids twittering round with cups of cocoa.

I had them all, and all appurtenances:
Frog's-spawn like tapioca, minnows darting,
Midges snap-gobbled up by cruising ducks,
A sudden flurry of feathers, a hoarse quack,
Blankets of pondweed, sticks, all kinds of muck.

The whole boiling in fact, to get *Magnet* back.

THE SCYTHER

'The young gentleman was up at six o'clock'
He said, stroking his scythe with the grey stone.
He smiled, and she smiled, and I who hadn't known
He'd seen me, blushed to the roots with the shock
Of his old burry voice finding me out of bed
So early. 'Seemed sort of hypnotised' he said.

Simply recalling something plays us tricks.
Is it true I remember looking down
On that world of dew and grass and his brown
Arm swinging? Or is it the image sticks
Because of what he said? I'll never know.
The grass falls. The sun rises. Days go.

THE DOUBLE

In my early teens I heard I had a double.
I never met him. In that decorous town
He did me a spot of harm. Always in trouble
He gave me a reputation I had to live down.

Something to do with girls — not me at all
(At that age anyway). A sad headmaster
Had a private word with Mr. and Mrs. Hall.
Their tolerance saved the family from disaster.

I often wonder what he was really like,
That identical boy — whether he knew of me
Taking the rap, riding round on my bike
Secretly proud of the devil I dared not be.

Perhaps we need a double to take the load
Of guilt we feel doing it on our own.
Better not meet him though. The shock might goad
One to a sort of murder, to be alone.

A VILLANELLE FOR KEITH DOUGLAS

Here on the title-page I read my name
In nine point. Above, three sizes larger, yours.
I feel like an interloper on your fame.

Have I a right to make this unwilled claim
On your estate, too late for your recourse?
Here on the title-page I read my name.

For how many misprints is my zeal to blame,
How many scholars you'd call crashing bores?
I feel like an interloper on your fame.

Yet inasmuch as we together came
At Oxford in Europe's last appalling pause
Here on the title-page I read my name.

Your frontispiece requires no hero's frame.
The desert's around you like a living force.
I feel like an interloper on your fame.

Though in that famous letter you exclaim
'We'll never accept each other's views, of course'
Here on the title-page I read my name.
I feel like an interloper on your fame.

GOING WRONG

Long before they took him away things were going wrong.
Simple things. Badly wrong. Like birds
Talking to him, not exactly with words
But a kind of language that wasn't song.

The very old get like this but he wasn't so old,
Sixty-odd only, a kind age
For many men with work opening its cage
And their children's children crossing the threshold.

Perhaps that was partly it — failure in all he'd done,
Career botched, no wife, child or home,
A bare existence in a barely furnished room,
Loneliness breeding a lust to be alone.

Where lonelier, then, than the far shores of the mind?
Slowly we watched him pulling out
Over those turbid waters, a growing doubt
Startling his eyes as he saw us left behind.

What he found on that continent we shall never know.
If only he'd send a message back
In a bottle for the tide to throw up like wrack,
We could go. Would go. But still we cannot go.

So they took him away and left us with this heart-ache
Of helplessness that a brain
Should be so wronged. Guilt, too, that we should stay sane —
As we must somehow, if only for his sake.

HIGH RISE

At three in the afternoon
On a weekday, being not at work,
I walk by the housing estate.
If I looked up and saw
The travelling clouds toppling
Those tall towers, I'd stumble
Myself with giddiness.

On the twenty-second floor
A young woman looks down
And discerns me, ant-size,
And the caterpillar trains
Weaving in over the points
To their roofed ends. A child whines
'Mum, can't I go out?'

I am afraid to look back
Or up or any way now.
I have suggested
A bundle falling and a small
Cry dying and the wail
Of the white van coming.
Suggestions are taken up.

HOME

Walking back on winter evenings
I pass a house where the curtains
Are never drawn. Some rangy house plants
Partly block the view, but peering
Between the leaves I surreptitiously discern
The lives of the four occupants.

They're lamplit as in a play, caught
In a family attitude. The mother
Has a child on her lap, one too
Kneeling beside her, her arms about
Their waists. If he's home, the father
Presides over the group. They view,

In a flickering white-blue element,
Whatever it is one views at six
With small children — puppets perhaps
Or cartoons or the latest instalment
Of a space fiction serial. The tricks
Amuse so, one of them actually claps.

It's almost as though the play of my life
Was being rehearsed. In my time,
Even my children's time, the distractions
Were only different in kind. Instead of live
Images, we pored over pictures in Grimm,
But essentially the attractions

Were the same — a going-to-bed
Routine of stories and small snacks,
A feeling of being cocooned
In a long heritage of childhood
That unconsciously carries one back
To a cave, rushlight, lullabies crooned.

With curtains drawn or undrawn, the street,
In private units, acts out this old
Mystery. I stride through its heart.
I open my door on a complete
Life — children grown-up, adult books. A cold
Wind blows in. It's home though. An ancient art.

DISCOVERING FLOWERS

For a full hour she scuttles about
Discovering flowers. From the edge of my eye
I watch, though seemingly lost in my book.
She's my willing distraction, I
A mere blob on the perimeter of things.
    Sometimes she sings.

What she brings back — buttercup, speedwell —
Is less for me than for the sake of the world
That's fêted her so. A simple child-way
Of thanking God or whoever unfurled
These amazing perspectives. She doesn't care
    Who — it's all there.

Is it without regret I open my book
In the historic present to find the flower
She brought me flattened, dead? Yes, I let go
That longing my mother had. The hour
Is spent. My child has run where she ran
    And copes as she can.

O HALF-WAY PLACES

You're consumed by distance.
India swallows you.
I don't know where you are.
You have not written.
Every morning I look
For your dart of daughterhood.

Your night's my day,
Your day's my night.
Timeless the airlines
Shuttle between us.
Somewhere our thoughts
Wing in to touch-down.

Across the Galata
I come to greet you.
We've left our shapes there.
O half-way places
Where love may gather
And be together.

THE CRAFT OF FICTION

There was a story he had to tell.
His publisher was waiting with a fat advance.
The trouble was, life was such hell
At home, what with the iced-lolly vans
And the Smiths breezing in and Top of the Pops
Blaring out, he hadn't a chance.

So he bought a cottage as far away
As he decently could without people imputing
He'd deserted his wife — out Newmarket way,
Rather flat, but then he wasn't commuting
For the sake of the view, just a friendly pub
Down the road and no cars hooting.

He furnished it cheaply without any guff.
A bed, a table and chair, some drawers for his clothes.
Frozen food mainly — fish-finger stuff —
Except for the freshly baked loaves
Old Miller still made in spite of the pap
Churned out by the bread-factory stoves.

Ideal, he thought. Now he could soldier on
Like a house on fire (odd saying, that —
He checked his insurance). By Chapter One
He'd manoevred his heroine into her hat,
Packed her off to a fancy dress ball,
And managed some tolerable chat.

Chapter Two and he'd lined up her lover.
A bit of a sweat getting his pedigree right
But he seemed to fit — neither too much above her
Nor beneath, a sort of middle-class knight.
And his rival? Someone plebeian goes well,
Say a bumped-up Battersea wight.

All set then. These three (whose names you should know,
Emily, Cedric and Jim) getting on fine,
In fact really running the show.
One doubt (as our author sits down to dine) —
Isn't a masterpiece *mastered*? Forget it.
Such veritas muddies the wine.

Emily washes, Cedric rather gingerly dries,
Jim puts away. Now time for charades.
Chapter by chapter they act out their lives.
Others enter and take up their parts.
He puts in the commas and crosses the t's
But lets them shuffle the cards.

So the personae grow. He builds on a wing,
Puts in a housekeeper and a girl for the chores.
He's almost finished the thing.
Chapter Twenty and the novel is yours.
But he'll stay with his household for ever,
The beauties and blackguards and bores.

The end of the story? Not quite, still five lines to go.
Proceedings have to be taken to bring him to heel.
Cruelty? Desertion? Too tricky and slow.
Adultery stinks, but thousands survive the ordeal.
Only one snag. That little note in his book:
All characters fictitious, none of the places are real.

IMPROPER USE

Give me patience, lord.
I make the same mistakes
Over and over again.
But if I pulled the cord
And you slammed on the brakes
And the whole buffering train

Ground to a halt, God knows
What spot we'd shudder to.
Those piles of waiting sacks
By ruled potato rows
Up the line from Crewe
And farms up rutted tracks

And a woman hanging out
Her smalls like help-me flags,
The vast unnerving silence,
The tiny hand-cupped shout
Of a labourer who gags
'Run out of juice?' and pylons

And twenty-five quid due
(Payable as under)
To the British Railways Board.
No, better to whistle through
Greater Boob and Blunder —
Given patience, lord.

OPUS 1

'Oh, go on, let me see it.' I surrender
A dark blue exercise book, ruled feint,
A little cracked down the spine. Half tender,

Half teasing, you enunciate my quaint
Once so serious phrases. Not what you'd choose!
Can it be, then, my generation went

A last ramble through Palgrave? All those O's
Apostrophising buds and birds and streams,
How they litter the pages — now, I suppose,

Impossibly archaic. Your voice seems
Faintly astonished that this style was me.
The room grows dark. An early headlamp gleams

On metal fittings, knobs, the still-blank eye
That entertains our evenings. Soon
Switches will swamp us. Child, how can you see?

'What's this?' Gently you laugh. You read: *O Moon.*

THE EYE

One night, one spring, he clambers on a chair
And clutches back the curtain. The garden waits
Darkly expectant, vigilants everywhere.
     Around the gate
A luminous foam of hawthorn loads the air
With too much sweetness. Senses suffocate.

Six Bramleys, drenched in blossom, smudge the gloom.
The grass bank falls towards the hidden stream
That knits two counties. Just below his room
     Two bushes seem
To lurk like assassins. A new-scythed fume,
Heady with sap, moithers him in its steam.

Nothing is real yet everything is real.
Time moves, stands still. The place is here and there,
A mix of visions. Ambiguous forces steal
     As leopards dare
Among the shadows. Mottled fingers feel
The velvet silences. Small creatures stir.

Nearby his parents sleep, mulling his years.
His brother, too, under the stooping eaves
Chugs through his infancy. And no one fears,
     Imagines or grieves
What fate this family holds. This night is theirs
Always — a long vigil no death bereaves.

One night, one spring, a memory will be born
Out of the latest death and all come back
Astonishing as a dream — brook, bank, and lawn,
     Even the thick
Effluvium of the may — clear as the dawn
He strains for now, this chilling on his cheek.

And so at last up the provincial sky,
Haloing spires and chimneys, like the rise
Of a low moon, that long-awaited eye
    Huge with surprise
Opens, unclouds, and swivelling round the grey
Garden, meets his expectant gaze, to recognise.

OLD PRINTS

They dream of another age,
    These exquisite views,
Leisurely carriages,
    A cobbled mews,
Cud-chewing Regency cows
    In pastures that look
Utterly changed now, boys
    Angling a brook.

How well they'd deceive us,
    These elegant scenes,
If they were our only clues
    To yesterday's means.
No-one, it seems, etched
    The back streets that ran
Just out of eye-shot, wretched
    With hunger and pain.

Art in its various uses
    Can only fulfil
Itself through the talents it chooses.
    Too gentle the skill
Of these local view masters,
    Too narrow their frames
For history's disasters,
    Humanity's shames.

TWO INKWELLS

Two inkwells. Empty. Victorian things.

A young girl sitting at a secretaire
Dips and pauses. How to put it? 'Sir.'
No, that won't do. Too formal. Would 'My dear'
Confuse the issue? Hardly. So . . . 'I fear,
'After much long and sympathetic thought,
'And caring for my dear parents as I ought
'(Father, I have to tell you, is much worse
'But cannot, alas, afford a proper nurse),
'I must refuse. I'm sensible of the pain
'This note will cause you. Believe me, I remain
'Most gratefully yours, Amelia.   P.S.
'To meet again would only cause distress.'
She smooths the blotter. An inquisitive eye,
Holding it to a mirror, might espy
How on this day in eighteen sixty-three
She locks a door and throws away the key.
Later, by poverty's ineluctable rules,
She hires her spinsterhood to small dame schools,
Unholidayed, unless of course you count
Wheeling a widower up and down the front
At Hove or Broadstairs, to augment her wage.
Edwardian shadows gather round her age.
A pistol shot! Old orders collapse like cards.
Nothing disturbs the geriatric wards.
Then as the Charleston jerks upon the scene
A trolley smoothly glides behind a screen.
Only a nephew sees the earth thud down
And calls the junk man in, gets half-a-crown.

O pen-poised moments! Our chances and refusings!

Two inkwells. Empty. Victorian things.

IN MEMORY OF WILLA MUIR
(d. May 1970)

A month late I heard,
    Asking for your address,
    That all your long distress
Was over. The exact date

I still don't know and now
    It doesn't matter much.
    You're out of sight and touch
And farther than I can go.

It seems so long since I
    Climbed down those narrow stairs
    To bring my small affairs
And listen to your strong

Not-to-be-broken voice.
    Though some were kept away
    By what you had to say,
I heard you softly-spoken,

Heard the tired crack that ran
    Through those articulate words
    And begged you afterwards
To tackle the journey back.

Thank God your strength held out
    To see you through that thing
    You aptly called *Belonging*;
For you were part at length

Not only of the fate
    Of your especial one
    But of the evil done
Through forty years by lonely

Wilful embittered men.
　　Those treacherous times you shared.
　　Kafka and Broch declared,
Through you, how few fulfil

The good we must suppose,
　　If we have any faith,
　　Each mortal sets out with
Though faltering on the road.

So you though not made 'beautiful
　　Or rare in every part'
　　Carried as good a heart
As you were meant to do.

And now your name with his
　　I put on the one shelf.
　　You did not spare yourself.
For the story's sake your frame

Though cruelly wronged lived out
　　Its last long-suffering span;
　　Then lay down by its man
Thankfully, and belonged.

PERSONS ONCE LOVED

Persons once loved are loved in a sense always.
They go yet never depart. Their times are driven
So deep we keep the occasions, like birthdays
That come round year after year though nothing's given.

Four or five women have cut their names in my heart.
Remembering one's not disloyal to the others.
The paradox is, however much they've hurt,
Or we've hurt them, they're still in a way our lovers.

Impossible not to wonder how they are
Or who they're with or whether our fashions linger
In what they do — like the ache of a limb not there
Or a wedding ring stuck fast on a widowed finger.

THE OLD CHANGES

Over fields and roofs
Bells float the years
As the sun drives
Shadows like slow spears

Deeper and deeper
Into the night.
Who is this half-sleeper
In the half-light

Listening as wood creaks
To the old changes?
Days drift with rooks
Down the darkening ranges.

A HOUSE OF VOICES

This year, my fiftieth, it seems I've travelled back
So often, revisiting those dead ones,
Those times and places that make up the memory-wrack
Of all my days. Surely I may be excused.
This, the first reading breath I drew for *Once*
Is being exhaled. It's a life-sigh being loosed.

I have come from a house where an assorted
Company warms up for tea. One, my step-grandmother,
Looks prim but is truly 'a good sort'.
Her husband, twinkling, is reined in by the ought
Of convention and her eye. One uncle, voted
A wash-out, peddles milk crates. Another,

Sad in insurance, secretly nurses
A First War wound. A crazy cousin, my only
Precursor in poetry, perfects, rather, the art
Of dropping bricks. A boy, impish, curses
This grown-up do. Now two maids, waxy
From kitchener heat and never going out

Except to evensong, carry in tea. The spoons
Are hallmarked for my drawer — and for two girls
Who peep in, half amused. Mask the eyes of one,
You might have my mouth; the other's mouth, my eyes.
So, locked on our frequencies — smiles, cheekbones, curls,
Such hints to remembering — no kinship dies.

Now we three stand where the sun conflates us
In its warm way. Shuttered, that house of voices.
Grassed over, the holes and hoop-marks of old games.
I look for sky-signs: cumulus, nimbo-stratus —
I never get them right. I await their choices.
What matters is what they bring us, not their names.

DATE DUE
